HOUSE OF MUSIC

Suzanne Swanson

LAUREL
POETRY
COLLECTIVE

ACKNOWLEDGMENTS

"Memory" was previously published in *Mankato Poetry Review* (May 1991) and in *The Part of Us that Craved the World*, chapbook published by Poetry Hostages (1995); "About My People" in *Grain* 20/3 (Fall 1992); "When the Music Stops" in *Minnesota Monthly* (October 1992); "This is a Real Dream" in *The Pegasus Review* (February 1992); "Empress Maple" in *The New Press Literary Quarterly* (Spring 1994); "Coming of Age" in *The Part of Us that Craved the World*; "Mindfulness" in *A New Name for the Sun* (Laurel Poetry Collective, 2003) and in *Water~Stone Review* 7 (Fall 2004); "The wedding dress is leaving" in *Pulling for Good News* (Laurel Poetry Collective, 2004); "Just This One" in *Love Letters*, chapbook published by Laurel Poetry Collective (February 2005); "Insomnia" published (in slightly different form) as a letter to the editor, *Minneapolis Star Tribune*, March 23, 2005; "Night Open" in *Bluefire* (Laurel Poetry Collective, 2005); "Why Not?" as a broadside published by Laurel Poetry Collective, 2003: Eileen O'Toole, graphic designer.

Epigraphs and other quoted excerpts: Tony Tost, "A Halo Best Described as Oceanic," from *Invisible Bride* (Lousiana State University Press, 2004); Philip Levine, "Silent in America," from *Not This Pig* (Wesleyan University Press, 1968); Franz Wright, "Thanks Prayer at the Cove," from *The Beforelife* (Alfred A. Knopf, 2004); Rita Dove, "Pastoral," from *Grace Notes* (W. W. Norton, 1989); Deborah Keenan, "Time & Love," from *Good Heart* (Milkweed Editions, 2003); Elaine Equi, "Destinations," from *Decoy* (Coffee House Press, 1994); Nor Hall, *Irons in the Fire* (Barrytown/Station Hill Press, 2002); Mei-Mei Berssenbrugge, "Alakanak Break-Up," from *Empathy* (Station Hill Press, 1989); Nazim Hikmet, "On Living," from *Poems of Nazim Hikmet*, trans. Randy Blasing and Mutlu Kunuk (Persea Books, 1994); Jane Hirschfield, "Three Times My Life Has Opened," from *The Lives of the Heart* (Harper Perennial, 1997); Rolf Jacobsen, "Truth," from *Night Open: Selected Poems of Rolf Jacobsen*, trans. Olav Grinde (White Pine Press, 1993).

Thank you to all the Laurels; especially to Yvette Nelson, Teresa Boyer, Kathy Peterson, and Su Smallen, who read versions of this manuscript; to Sylvia Ruud, who designed this book. To Eileen O'Toole who made "Why Not?" into art. To Nor Hall, who imagined me a poet; Jim Moore, who treated me as one; and Deborah Keenan—one smart woman—as poet, teacher, friend.

© 2005 Suzanne Swanson
All rights reserved.
ISBN 0-9761153-4-4
Printed in the United States of America.
Published by Laurel Poetry Collective
1168 Laurel Avenue, St. Paul MN 55104
www.laurelpoetry.com
Book design by Sylvia Ruud

Library of Congress Cataloging-in-Publication Data

Swanson, Suzanne, 1948–
    House of music / Suzanne Swanson
      p. cm.
    ISBN 0-9761153-4-4
    I. Title.
PS3619.W3636H68 2005
811'.6—dc22

2005012819

*For my families
— all their songs*

CONTENTS

Somewhere on Summit   11

I. *...desire, and the freedom to imagine it*

Thin, Common   15

Equation   17

Question   18

About My People   19

When the Music Stops   20

Toward Home   21

The wedding dress is leaving   22

This is a real dream   23

eyes-straight-ahead   24

What They Were Made Of   25

Again, Again   26

We could not recognize the world   27

II. *Whatever we had believed in hadn't crushed us yet...*

Memory	31
Peach	32
How I Learned	33
Evidence	34
In the Present	35
Chopin	36
Our Own	37
How I Learned	38
Easter	40
The Way the Spring Wants	41
Great Gray	42

III. *This romance of going from city to city with a lamp*

John Renbourn's Guitar	45
Rummage	46
She is swaddled, patient.	47
Beautiful Sky	48
Summer again and the jealousy of time.	49
Coming of Age	50
After Weeping	51
Insomnia	52
All Cellos	53
i realize again that water is god	54
Empress Maple	55

What Now?	56
A Thing Held Close	57
Finally	58
Guest House	60
Past Me	61

IV. *Do we have joy in this field?*

Night Open	65
That Would Be Love	66
Interlude, Erasure	67
January Ice	68
Question, February	69
Just This One	70
Desire, Small	71
Invasion	72
After Joining	73
Mindfulness	74
What does the accordion do?	75
Fooled	76

Why Not?	79

> *Lord,*
> *I make up nothing*
> *not one word.*
>
> —Franz Wright, "Thanks
> Prayer at the Cove"

Somewhere on Summit

she said *evil*, repeated it later
in writing. This was after I said *poignant*. About
what? Something between absence and solitude,
the filling of space, permission denied.

There is work and there is work. Not asking
for relief. Release, then? How to distinguish?
Evil not to make the effort to distinguish.
Evil to craft of memory psychic truth.

Poignant how we make of our walk and talk
and despair and foul weather a lattice: grief
and love.

—for Deborah Keenan

I

...desire, and the freedom to imagine it.

—Rita Dove, "Pastoral"

Thin, Common

> *I shall be transported to the river above or the river below*
> —Tony Tost

1.
She sits in September, surrounded by books until she reads Philip Levine—*but I have found I am where/I am by/being only there,/by standing/in the clouded presence of/the things I observe*—and she is released to cut the last bouquets of summer: black-eyed Susans, brown-eyed Susans, asters, oregano, Russian sage, two tiny sweet peas.

2.
She places them in water, allows them to arrange an outdoor room. The wind tries to stop time. In the water the cut flowers are moving from one state to another. They have this in common with almost everything, including the morning glories still erasing their trellis.

3.
You must study transportation, the coming in, the going out, respiration, its pauses, the weather that binds one season to another.

4.
This morning:
    Brave blue sky. Autumn
    Hammers pounding. Roofs ready
    For winter's halo.
By afternoon, only the sound of waves of air breaking against the highest branches—that and the crows' alarum.

5.
The storm arrives. Vases topple. The view now aslant. At the Mississippi, the rain lifts, the sky divides, crisp and thin, as if

spread with voile: blue below; above, dove gray. Water lights on air lights on water.

6.
Every cell breathes.
Every tributary flows into the heart's ocean.

Equation

the body a closet
      light closes around an interior
   heart so close to spine
        closest of all to breath and breathing
no breath: closure's
  mirage, a closet for time
       cloisonne, brilliance

Question

Where, flax, do you find
your color? the blue I count a patchwork

memory of field and water
and sky, every summer-

time trip to St. Hilaire, the packed
Plymouth paralleling the Red River

of the North, me catching
through the rolled-down window at least

a glimpse // unravelling blur //
of my heaven.

About My People

1. One Side

Name the tractors, build
the barn before the house.
Walk 5 miles to school, save
for a piano. When the house burns down,
save again. Plant honeysuckle
outside the front door no one ever uses.
Feed families of stray
cats, give your dogs the same
name for 25 years, don't
smile, put up plums, put up
your hair in braids every morning, die
because you don't believe
in doctors.

2. The Other

Free land? Pack up, drive north
for days. Begin to know
the meaning of "ours."
Whistle your children home. Knead
12 loaves at a time in the old
dishpan. Buy a canary, order
your underwear from the Monkey Ward
catalog. Till a garden bigger
than the house. Render hogfat
into lard. Watch for the first
black-eyed Susans. Milk, and milk, and
milk the cows. Never say
death. Never die.

When the Music Stops

The preachers in his little country
across the sea said "no dancing,"
so he sailed away, found my grandmother
landlocked, and waltzed her
into nine children. When she died,
he lasted one winter in their house.
In April the creek began to run and he
sold the farm. Said, "I never made
one step on this prairie without her.
I'm not about to start now."

Toward Home

Black horse in a winter field.
Mozart sparkling.
Your syncopated heart
an engine. Our bed, the boat.
Western sun presses
at my back.

The wedding dress is leaving

the dream. She is tired
of being compared to the gewgawed
cake, even if it is true, she is too full

of frills and bric-a-brac
she did not choose herself.
The designer set aside sophistication
so the innocent bride would fall in love

with the proper fantasy. This causes the wedding
dress to sigh. In her own view,
the Platonic version of her substance
is truly narrow, an aesthetic that allows

even the naif's body to call out
for hand on veiled shoulderblade, hip to hip.
So she is leaving the dream
now, tugging her dreamer into another set

of symbols, another knowledge. What will emerge
when she has dragged the dreamer
into the thicket and refuses to come out?

This is a real dream

A couple in their 50s
sit in their local cafe. She
picks at her meatloaf. He wolfs
down his mashed potatoes. Over
the years their bodies have come
to resemble each other. They both
wear black satin bowling jackets.
The embroidery is red. They never
look at each other.

He goes to make a phone call.
This phone is special. It records
his message, then sends him back
to the table. The special phone
calls his wife. She is surprised,
and acts it. What she hears
is, "I love you," no buzzing,
no hum. Her face has fallen into
the shining expectancy of youth,
as her husband sits there pale, trying
around his mouth not to show he is affected.

eyes-straight-ahead

that sports car
        motor racing
                idling fast

it wasn't you

                sleek
stereotype of sex

       and power

through the headlights'
metal covers

you see   how
      if it was clear

      straight out
the speedometer
            blurring

your eyes blown into

            and disturbed

What They Were Made Of

Even though we weren't agreed
about the position of heaven, we began

to think about God. We wondered: are clouds
religious? We watched them shade

the moon, go up against the sun
in friendly sport. Sometimes they

would enter our bodies, shift
around organs and molecules, make us

as expansive as hope. They told us
they were made of water

and desire. We believed them,
watching ourselves settle

into pools of longing.

Again, Again

A woman. It is her job to pull back the hand on the clock
as it nears twelve, the big hand, back always to eleven,

five-minutes-to, back to "almost." It's been like that, too,
in this confounded marriage. Remember that group we tried

so long ago? Everybody else got better, all the other couples
made all the right moves and we were an embarrassment.

Once I was stupid, brought in a little paragraph I loved—
Henry Miller on the light in Greece. Greece, that light

where I conceived one child, carried another. Their voices
clouded and strained. They chastened me for hiding.

"Don't you have words of your own?" Then "Yes and no,"
I wanted to say, "these *are* my words now.

Miller found the raw material, worked it into treasure."
It was the wrong place, our troubles stone

compacted to harder stone. I stand here, Mediterranean heart
in a pale body, the hour so close. I can't find Miller any more,

those words are lost. Someone else must speak for me again.

"There is a door. It opens. Then it is closed. But a slip of light
    stays, like a scrap of unreadable paper left on the floor,
    or the one red leaf the snow releases in March."

      [last three lines from the poem "Three Times My Life Has Opened,"
      by Jane Hirschfield]

We could not recognize the world

All the cardinals hidden

We wrote poems in long-lined stanzas
Abstract words abounded, sung arias to one another
It made us tired to write them, tireder still to read
We forgot about red

Still present and erased into streaks of gray

November comes and gray is our watchword
We forget how it can fog an entire morning in May
How it belongs to our gladness
Watching life shift in and out of view

II

*Whatever we had believed in
hadn't crushed us yet…*

—Deborah Keenan, "Time & Love"

Memory

The frog's eye sees

the fly, and with just that
image on the retina, the tongue

can snap it into immediate
food. The brain is not

included in the transaction.
What is it for, then?

The Greeks said,
to cool the blood.

Left to the heart alone,
wouldn't we all combust—one

memory after the other driving
our temperatures beyond recognition?

Peach

As a boy, I'd still have wondered how that baby
got inside, how it breathed, what made it turn
into a little brother or sister.

I wouldn't have found the answers in my father's
lower left-hand drawer, home to the book of men's questions,
the book with the girly peach paper cover cupping
a sobered version of pleasure and reassurance:
"many a young man
has gotten lost in the rosettes
of the vulva on his wedding night."

There were line drawings, too, I think, but
I might not remember them if I'd been a boy,
either.

How I Learned

1. It was a completely different
time. My father knew. My mother

had her babies fast. He left us—
my brother and me—on the hospital lawn.

We played under the oaks.
We never thought of safety:

it was our town, it was our hospital. We stayed
right where he told us. Once

he came to say we had a baby brother.
We were happy. We played some more.

We were not allowed inside.

2. Our mother came home
in the car. She carried a bundle

of blue and white receiving blankets with a squishy
little face. We bounced in the back

trying to see it. In the living room,
she sat in the big fuzzy chair. The face

began to make faces. It snuffled. She
opened her blouse. Something very, very brown

peeked out. It looked like maybe an animal—
a nose, an ear? She showed it to our baby,

and he liked it. He licked it, and was quiet.

Evidence

I mean living must be your whole occupation
— Nazim Hikmet

A cemetery—why here
is burial allowed
only for infants?

The heaven of water
washing time, pushing time
into evidential hillocks
on the far shore

Embroidery: color
as a means
to defy gravity

Rudimentary knowledge
of another language // cracking
open the bound world

Grief as surprise,
surprise as grief

No, it is not possible to hear
Mendelssohn
without thinking happily of your brother
and the crow
and the Fingal's Cave cartoon.

In the Present

This morning my son pointed out
the early sky. He requires
impressive beauty. He wasn't ashamed to want
his mother to see what he loves:
pink, so alive it was almost fuschia,
splitting the safe blue-gray
cover of morning like the pink
of membranes, the underside of a tongue,
swollen labia. Like a lung surviving
on its own, happily removed from its cave.
Arousal. He is on the edge of that thought,
but the precipice remains invisible. For a time
we can still gaze together
at the fierce and palpable dawn.

Chopin

lassoes the sixteen-
year-old boys, commands
and champions them.
Their hands tremble
for their turn
at the piano. We say *power*, we say
testosterone—and also they cannot wait
to rattle the keys
of romance, to translate yearning
into volume and arpeggio,
to drift, unanchored boat, over love's
musical waters, then
to storm through them, bound
to the time
signature's mast.

Our Own

We rode into it, right there beside the grain elevator.
Summer and we prayed each in our own religion
for full sun by one PM, free swim time, so the pool could open.
We put on our admission pins, knotted towels
around our waists—each one too big, in our opinion—and met
at the usual corners, pumped our bicycles—Schwinns,
a Husky, and my moss-green mongrel—to the little store
for red licorice and Black Jacks, and got back on. Across Hiawatha
at St. Leo's, a funny feeling in our chests and I saw it
first, the scalloped sheet of rain and shadow advancing
on our girl cadre, and we sped up, rode straight for it, right there
beside the grain elevator, squealing and swerving, ducking
our heads and then swinging them back to catch the fat drops
in our mouths, shaking our wet hair, no-hands,
as the sun shot through the gray and made our little town
look like a God-picture hung on the basement wall of First Lutheran
or Kathy's church or Julie's or the other Suzanne's, and God was good,
we had been given what we needed, given nature and bodies
and full-size bikes with 26-inch tires to ride toward whatever was next.

How I Learned

1. Owning Up

I am in love with capital S's. The hard work
it takes to make them, nothing straight
about them, how you have to try
to keep the upper curve smaller
than the lower, even when you print.

And the cursive, how it leans
and swirls. How S can look almost
like a swan, the bird gracefully swimming
in my name.

S is my letter.

It's wrong, I know, to call attention
to myself, to be so proud, so happy
in possession. But God was the one
who let me be born in September. How
can He be mad I love my initials
when He gave the same ones
to Sunday School, the place
I go to worship Him, the place I go
to learn how to be good?

2. Never, Ever

She twirls into dizziness
in her new dress, the one
the neighbor's daughter outgrew.

The skirt waves a circle of indigo
plaid around her waist.
A skirt made for a little girl

who loves herself. She knows
from Sunday's sermon

this should never happen.
Her body does not care,
spins over the rules, spins beyond.

Easter

After church, the girl wanders
away from her aunt's house.
She climbs to the top of the rise.
Across two hills a white horse
gallops, fenceless. She forgets
her fear of what is large,
her aversion to lack of color. She tries
to hear it whicker. She sees herself
mount the horse and ride,
as unfettered as Jesus rolling away the stone.

The Way the Spring Wants

> ...*the nervous pressure of light*
> —Mei-Mei Berssenbrugge

The way the spring wants
not to crystallize into
summer, not to be that much
closer to the opposite side
of the year, for the idea
of color to remain
only a petal pressed
between the pages of a hymnal.

The way the swallow swerves
from a straight path, dipping
toward the earth in remembrance
of the fall, shying from
the threshold that insists
on tracking the sun.

The way the trees send
a whisper down the boulevard
in the gray breeze, seal
their leafy lips, stand
upright and casual as spies.

Great Gray

Believe it—sixty-two
owls.

Cramped hours in the little car.

Still—*oh* escapes
at every sighting.

Pale pewter sky
on snow: dull light
and dark and no shadow.

The dish of the great gray wheels
on its axis
when it wants to
absorb us—
cocks forward to apprehend
the vole
beneath its snow.

This day is timeless.
Everything can reach us now.

III

*This romance
of going from city to city
with a lamp.*

— Elaine Equi, "Destinations"

John Renbourn's Guitar

Sun breaks through
      clouds just like
           the sun breaking
                through the clouds

And God is there
    just
        like God

I drive on and on
      beneath
          that sky

Rummage

I am opening and closing closet doors, peeking into jewelry boxes and trunks. I am scouring the house for any trinket someone else might buy. My daughter's class needs money. I'm divesting myself for her. She's thirteen and bound for places designed to stir the blood. If she could, she'd go without the physical presence of adults, only their love in the form of cash and tired good wishes. Some days, though, as lost in her new body as I am in mine, she wants me, her old home. Some days she fools us both into believing we are the creatures we were not so long ago, offers me her heart, that most indefinite possession, the one which can only be given, not given away, never sold, no purchase gained. Comes to me carrying the small heart that galloped first in my thick redness.

She is swaddled, patient.

I pick her up. The infant eyes
lock mine. I remember
that she belongs
to the house of music
and I carry her there.

Beautiful Sky

Blue wraps a phantom
cello, stray cloud-wisps skitter
across piano keys.

The bass pulses, beams
stand-up sun. Cool prairies warm.
Bells, snares: sunset, dawn.

Now a saxophone—
alto—and again . . . time's drift
from earth to heaven.

>   —after Ellen Lease's "Beautiful Sky" for jazz quartet

Summer again and the jealousy of time.

Without a mirror, I see my face

smudged into one of a hundred greens. I will
the body's loss, no line

between awkward July's breeze and my slow
skin. Today I know that sun

and rain love one another. Today I see
how much they are willing to give

away, sacrifice just to keep a season fresh,

just to quiet my foolish mouth.

Coming of Age

The mirror catches
my face.
My mother's mother
glances back. Not just age.
Not just starry lines
and eggplant
eyes. Now her countenance
commands
my features, insists
on sculpting a droop
into my cheek, as if
I had been born
her raw material,
waited
my entire
young life
to belong to her.

After Weeping

How
small
her dream: the stage,
its little
velvet
midnight
curtain.

In a half-
moon,
the audience,
eyes
on
each other's mouths.

Insomnia

You're in the car. The landscape turns foreign, you can't place it, no room for sheer absence. On Pascal Avenue, four stumps sit like enormous fungi, ashamed. More on St. Clair at the rise of the hill. More everywhere. They bring out stories of the first wave years ago. Tears, always, and loneliness, still, for our elms. How can we sleep for thinking of the empty spaces, how do we breathe deep and slow, minus their hovering?

All Cellos

are loyal to satin
and the blue of a northern

sea. They swallow dusk
and live on midnight.

They hover at death's
bedside: all cellos know

which last chord to play.
All cellos were born

ambulatory. Even when
their notes are written

with wings, all four strings
ablur, all cellos balance

on the round beats
of our hearts. They anchor

summer's balloon with autumn's
circular moans. They maroon us—

cellos do—where we do not wish
to be found.

i realize again that water is god

a hut in the woods
  dark remembered   night's belly
moonless sky swallows

the world's largest
        lake   lost, i advance
        like one
felled by grief
                each foot hopes
to toe gravel   corrects
      for earth

at the road's
meadow
      stars
            the voices

of waves   faithfulness

their demand

Empress Maple

The cold sun shifts the shadows
of remnant leaves. The Empress Maple
perseveres, last to shimmer
green against the wind. Just before
its final shudder, the tree
is yellow lace.

How we have persisted, determined
to forestall winter
with the force of our brightness.

What Now?

In her sleep, raccoons, jaunty, indifferent to the point of cruelty.
They weigh on her all day, their little bandit stares.
She would like much less visibility.
She would rather approximate energy than matter.
She would rather appear in the appling autumn air as an aroma.
She could be a desire just beyond words.
She has lost half her heart to longings like these, reveries dolled up
    in smart hope.
She wants now to be bald, tattered, stop sweeping up messes.
Leave the garbage where it's tossed.
Give the animals access, let them use their craft, get what they can.

A Thing Held Close

The bodyworker lives on the river.
All through the session, a tapping

of fish mouths on the hull. They want algae.
I want my neck to move. I barely know

what she does with me ~
hands, her smoky breath,

puffs, a click. I see I must lay it down,
a thing I have held close. Like the mother

howler, who carried her injured infant
even after the flies lit, and after days

laid his matted body across a tree limb,
but kept and kept his hand in hers,

then let it go and covered her own eyes
well into the night.

Finally

My mother lets me know
they are prepared. She tells me
my father has entered a list
of all the important numbers
in the new computer and also
tucked them away on actual paper
in the file marked Death.

I am of two minds:
1) OK. I want the tea kettle
when she is gone.
2) It will never happen.

I think maybe
the two are not mutually exclusive.
Sometimes I still believe
my grandfather is slurping his coffee
from the saucer, listening to Paul Harvey
on the radio. I just haven't gotten up there
to see him lately. Or he is an angel, flying tandem
with my grandmother, their wings
pink with the good fortune
of finding each other one more time.

I'm not ready for anything
permanent. It's almost too much
to notice the papery spots
on my father's face, to count how many
blood pressure pills my mother swallows.
I think of my children's births, the slow
crossing of a boundary
between nothing and something,

how they fell into this life,
into hands poised to catch them.

At seventeen I formulated my theory
of personal reality: stretches of deprivation
and distress punctuated by brief bursts
of pure happiness. Now I might say—
ashes, then a quick, hot fire. At the end,
will it be different for me, for the ones I love,
the flames finally refusing
to burn themselves out?

Guest House

We are asleep in the corner room, my sister next to me rooted to her bed, our father across from us makes his night noises. I am in the middle twin, my mother across the parking lot in Critical Care. The hospital calls her "asleep." I know that kind lie—she has landed in a world empty of time, full of forgetting. Sometimes her face is placid, sometimes the torture of recovery arches her frame. We are all happy now. My father's prayer before surgery introduced her to God: "I'd like to express my gratitude for Evelyn, my wife…" Later he promised to sing for her "How Deep Is the Ocean" (his single voice taking on all the barbershop chords). His love is deep, formal, contained. When we hear that her heart is back to beating, her lungs filling without a machine, some of us sob with the surprise of our own held breaths. He puts down his pencil, bows his head, returns to the crossword. All night now I dream of confinement. Toward morning, new material: a hazy figure crosses the room, opens a window over our heads.

Past Me

I am your frosted windowpane.
Look through me to see, after these many years, November
as more than brown, carrying on its hillsides
and fields and ditches grasses of lavender and orange, the red
of the highbush cranberry.

Look past me. Ask the rusty bell to sing.

IV

Do we have joy in this field?

— Nor Hall, *Irons in the Fire*

Night Open

Right there
inside
my breast, a bird
of paradise.
Flower
all angular
tropic and color.
With each breath
plumper, more ready
to fly.

I am like everyone else.
I want to fly.

I want its bluefire
blue, its green
rocking
cradleboat
(leaf-green) and the spiked
topknot orange
fingers
that will wave
hello
but not shyly,
that call *look, look here, look
at me in this body, swift
and swooning.*

> *What do you do? If you open/it will change your life.*
> —Rolf Jacobsen

That Would Be Love

Loneliness,
but
bracketed
by Morning
after Morning
of God's attempt
to show you
the Sun.

Interlude, Erasure

A hard freeze last night, and the tenderest flowers, color sustained by moisture and ongoing hope, have turned grotesque. This morning becomes an extension of Calvino's story of how to capture and kill—spread birdlime on the roof —which he appears to not think of as killing at all. The daughter wants the hummingbird for her hat—she must have it. She shall. Which variety, though? The mind manufactures its own image—our own ruby-throated—but this is not Italy. We are distraught in red and green. Perhaps we should be mourning copper and blue. Today's paper mentions three times that a female soldier has been killed in Tikrit. Is "she" erased if she is "soldier"? I will pull up the impatiens, toss their transparent stalks and their wedding petals into the compost. Already I am waiting for the sun, swallowed, to return.

January Ice

Morning car-pool. As usual, Xander flicks on the oldies. He's just turned eight, wants to know where he's come from. We've been through the Zombies to the Beatles when he wonders whether KOOL 108 might not play "Wowie Zowie" next. Oh, I doubt it, I tell him, but the other kids in the car don't know the song, want to know why, don't see why. It's my fault. My explanation pales and slips. How do you explain Frank Zappa? Why he's not an oldie, even though he's dead. I've drilled my children in the names of Frank's kids—Moon Unit, Dweezil. Music, names, it all counts, doesn't it? Maybe even simple appreciation saves my ordinary life from sliding into too ordinary. Now it makes me happy—blessed, simple, ordinary state—that my youngest launches into "It Can't Happen Here" and I join him, drowning out Gary Lewis and the Playboys, both of us haphazardly hammering away at those crazy dissonances Frank intended for the HERE at the end of every line, and we're right here, right now, today, rounding the snowy curve of Como Lake, right on track.

Question, February

I watch for some sign.
    The weather warms
        Into dirty gray—no snow.

A week, and the sky breathes
    Ice, indifferent,
        Fracturing. A horizon

At every degree of this circle, but
    Where to enter it? How
        To walk toward its distance?

You'll have to be my day-
    Star. You will be
        My night's cool moon.

Just This One

Satisfaction is September's
demand and right. No other month

> bracketing cicadas. Yesterday
> she said *I am pretty sure*

God wants me to write poetry and
you gasped and turned.

> Now the sky is thick
> with emptiness and generosity. It flows

down to you shaped like the wind
and just this one day you are

> alight and embedded. Today
> you—a grown woman—can be more

than half-alive without
the touch of another human being.

Desire, Small

Ten years ago you saw nature
split: sun sizzled into ocean,
moon grazed the tips
of mountain pine.
The same moment
to your right, to your left.

Your head hurt. You were alone.
You were happy.
You want it to happen again,
that caught-between
beauty, deft elegance
of up and down, look either way,
the stark immediacy
that only-one is a lie.

You can put that one
little enlightenment beside
your others: Wind/Canoe Taking on Water
and Selby Bridge at Sunset,
put them all in the category called life-
death, eternity-now—it is the smashedupness
that matters, that's the point
on which we rest, the world
in which we all turn, each
little history rubbing
up against the next.

Can you get it back
again: a leaf
just a leaf,
the storm simply rain
and wind, a little hail.
Can you?
Do you want to?

INVASION

They come from the far north.
They don't know roads.
They don't know cars.

This one we found on the snowy shoulder, great gray wing cocked.
My son understands these things:
Someone would be interested in DNA, facial feather patterns.

He got back in the car, held it
On his lap. It seemed as though we were in a room
With royalty. Not, though,

To the retriever, who believed the owl's turning
Aroma to be just about like that
Of any other dead bird.

After a while, we found a tiny general store,
Bought a roll of plastic bags and twist-tied one around
The corpse—its velvet, its shield. The dog stopped

Squeaking and crying and made her circle in the back.
We talked quietly about where to take the frozen body,
An ordinary conversation and an homage, too.

After Joining

What she wonders about still
is Jesus. His chutzpah. His riddles and demands.

The healing (all that casting out suspect
and attractive). She does not like

to call him Son. Where
did his body come from,

who does it belong to?
Sometimes he does appear

to manifest the sacred, a presence
like the omphalos at Delphi,

that time she heard the flute
no one was playing.

Sometimes he is just one more
good boy confused about power.

Nonetheless, she has begun to say
his name, started to stay still,

her eyes closed, but roaming,
roaming.

Mindfulness

I'm gobbling my Chinese take-out, little bits of chicken on my clean sweater. I'm trying to remember what that book on mindfulness said, something about non-doing, something about savoring every morsel—time or fried rice. But here's the thing: I kind of like the jazzed-up-ness of my body going a little too long without food, the mind-buzz, too. Remember Gena Rowlands in *A Woman Under the Influence*? Our common language stuck in my craw, but she may have heard my danger call. That scene where she flat-out goes crazy and starts to stretch out her neck and her hands like some battered bird who wants to move away, away, but she's on the top of a table so that just about anywhere she goes, actually, she's going to fall. It was like looking into a hidden mirror, the kind you find at the bottom of a story. The words repeat, they roll over each other like marbles. I won't stop talking. I won't.

What does the accordion do?

Stops and starts.

Surprises in the pause.

Coaxes one tone to mix with its neighbors—friendly, hostile.

Allows two notes—three?—to hang in suspension with despair, stir frenzy.

Demands the ear fly to polka, tango, monkey in the street.

Wraps around the shoulders of the clarinet, a shawl.

Squeezes air, pleat by pleat, into steps, ladders for those who have lived underground too long.

Fooled

Never a breeze. The devil believes
in stock-stillness

not the still of breath, the bellows
of quiet. That he curses: "may

rocks gather deep
in their lungs" he spits

as he watches the meditators
and the yoga class. Doesn't

waste his time
on Tai Chi or Qi Gong.

The devil likes
the concrete, wants everything dead

and alive stuck
fast. Thought the game of

Statue might be a paean
to him, banged

his head against a stop
sign when he realized

what a thrilling time they were having,
just waiting to spin

the next round.

Why Not?

Azure. You love it. No apologies.
Swathe the sleek sky. Toss it

into a lake at midmorning. Noon,
follow with the Atlantic. Wear it,

badge of your willingness to swoon, to shine
small against nature.

Press it onto an ancient black-
and-white photo, reinvent

contrast, blow the breath of stars
into the dead.

SUZANNE SWANSON's work has appeared in a collaborative chapbook, *The Part of Us That Craved the World*, and in several literary journals, most recently, *Water~Stone*. She is a recipient of the Loft Mentor Series Award. A psychologist specializing in pregnancy and postpartum, and a mother of three, she lives, works, and walks in St. Paul, Minnesota.

LAUREL POETRY COLLECTIVE

A gathering of twenty-three poets and graphic artists living in the Twin Cities area, the Laurel Poetry Collective is a collaboration dedicated to publishing beautiful and affordable books, chapbooks, and broadsides. Started in 2002, its four-year charter is to publish and celebrate, one by one, a book or chapbook by each of its twenty-one poet members. The Laurel members are: Lisa Ann Berg, Teresa Boyer, Annie Breitenbucher, Margot Fortunato Galt, Georgia A. Greeley, Ann Iverson, Mary L. Junge, Deborah Keenan, Joyce Kennedy, Ilze Kļaviņa Mueller, Yvette Nelson, Eileen O'Toole, Kathy Alma Peterson, Regula Russelle, Sylvia Ruud, Tom Ruud, Su Smallen, Susanna Styve, Suzanne Swanson, Nancy M. Walden, Lois Welshons, Pam Wynn, Nolan Zavoral.

For current information about the series—including broadsides, subscriptions, and single copy purchase—visit:

www.laurelpoetry.com

or write:

Laurel Poetry Collective
1168 Laurel Avenue
St. Paul, MN 55104